Earth and Space

Sally Hewitt

Chrysalis Children's Books

First published in the UK in 2003 by
Chrysalis Children's Books
64 Brewery Road,
London N7 9NT

ISBN 1 84138 688 X

British Library Cataloguing in Publication Data for this book is available from the British Library.

A Belitha Book

Editorial Manager: Joyce Bentley
Senior Editor: Sarah Nunn
Project editor: Jean Coppendale
Designers: Rachel Hamdi, Holly Mann
Illustrators: Kevin Maddison, Lisa Smith and Gwyneth Williamson
Educational consultants: Sally Morgan and Helen Walters

Printed in China

Contents

Words in **bold** are explained in the Glossary on pages 30-31.

Life on Earth

The planet we live on is called Earth. Our nearest star is the sun. Warmth and light from the sun make it possible for plants and animals to live almost everywhere on Earth.

Many animals live on the land
Land
Sheep
Cows
Horse
Insects fly through the air
Ducks
Bumble bees
Seagull
People
Sand
Butterfly
Poppies
Grasshopper
Nettles
PICTURE SEARCH
★ look for plants and animals on land
★ look for plants and animals in the air
★ look for plants and animals in the water – remember people are also animals.

Planet Earth

Planet Earth is surrounded by layers of **air**, called the atmosphere. Most plants and animals need air to live.

Earth and the *seasons*

Earth spins round and round in space.
As Earth spins, it **orbits** – which means it moves around the sun.

A year

The Earth takes just over a year, 365¼ days, to orbit the sun.

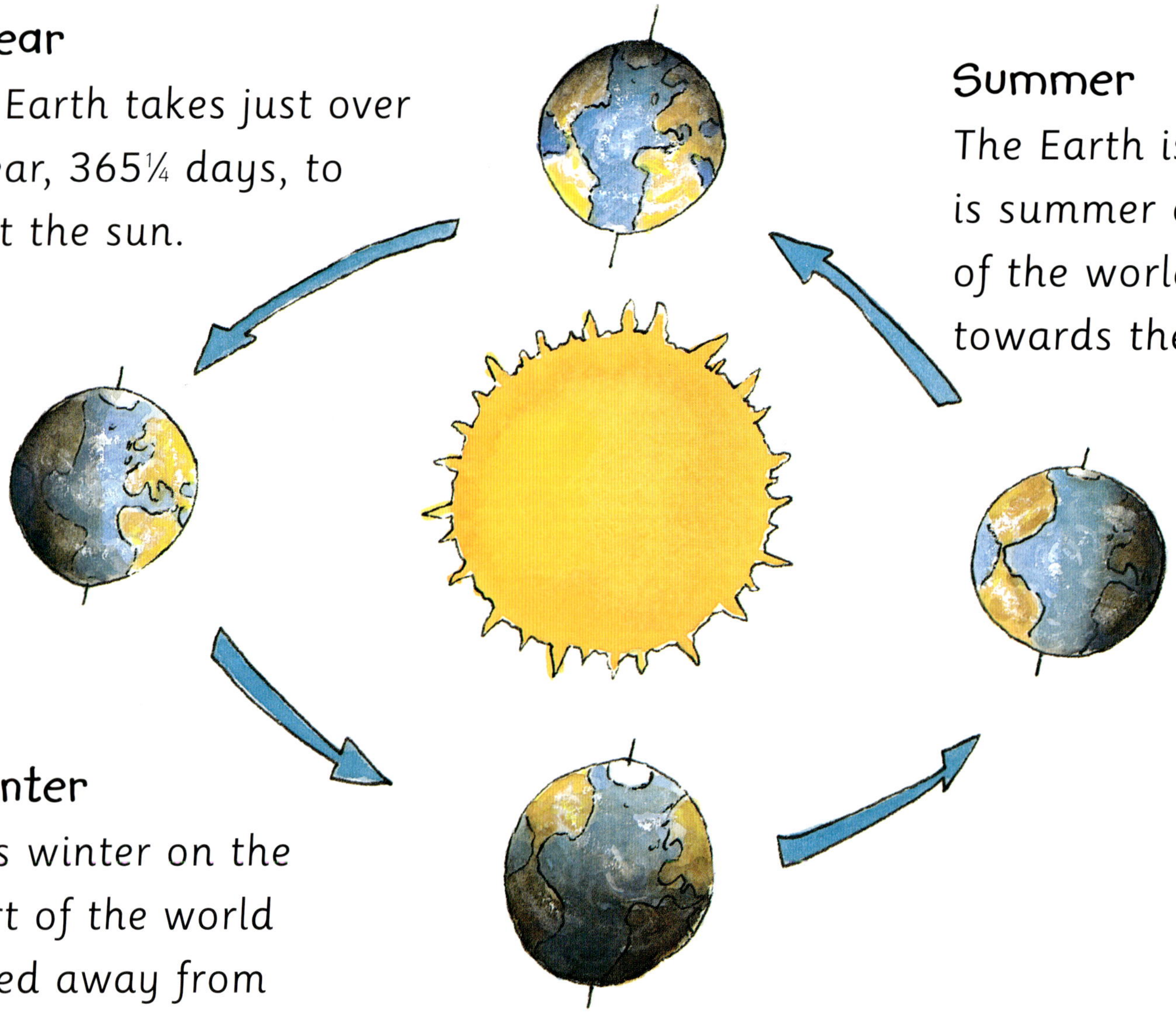

Summer

The Earth is **tilted**. It is summer on the part of the world tilted towards the sun.

Winter

It is winter on the part of the world tilted away from the sun.

Day and night

Earth takes a day, or 24 hours, to spin around once. It's daytime on the part of the Earth facing the sun, and it's night time on the part in shadow.

SHADOWS

On a sunny day, ask a friend to draw around your shadow in the morning. Stand in the same position at midday. Ask your friend to draw around your shadow again. Then do the same in the afternoon.

What has happened to your shadow? How has it changed size and shape from the morning to the afternoon?

MAKE A MODEL OF THE EARTH

1 Mix 2 tablespoons of PVA glue with 2 cups of water. Tear 2 sheets of newspaper into short strips.

2 Scrunch another sheet of newspaper into a ball and push a stick through the middle.

3 Now dip the strips of newspaper in the glue mixture. Stick them on the ball in layers.

4 When the ball is dry, paint it to look like the Earth. Draw a line around the middle – this is an imaginary line called the equator.

5 In a dark room, turn on a lamp to act as the sun. Tilt your model of the Earth and move it around the lamp. See how the light shines on the bottom half and then shines on the top half as you move the model around.

Land and sea

Earth is like an enormous ball made up of layers. The very outside layer is called the **crust**. The crust is the land we live on and is surrounded by sea.

PICTURE SEARCH

- ★ look for all the different colours of rock
- ★ look for all the different colours of sand and soil

Seas and oceans

The Earth's surface is shaped into mountains, **valleys** and **plains**. Almost three quarters of the Earth's surface is covered by seas and oceans.

Fossil

This **fossil**, found in chalk cliffs, is the remains of a sea creature. It died millions of years ago.

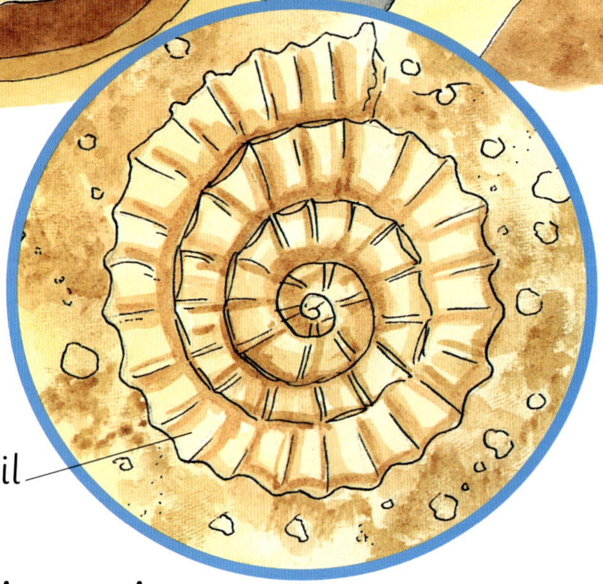

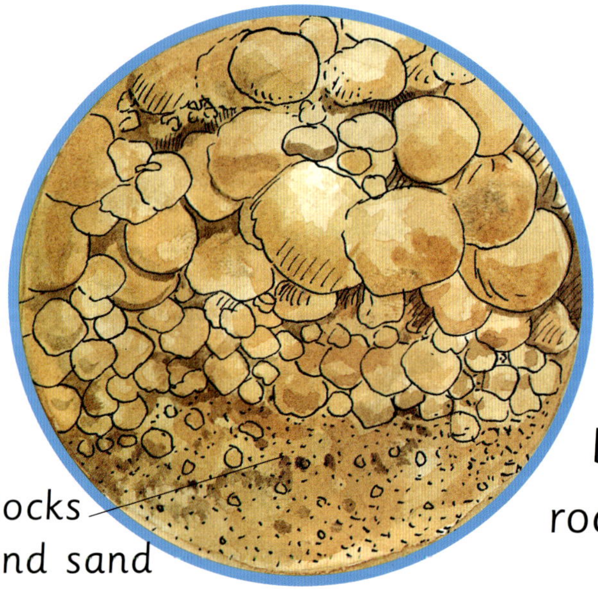

Rocks and sand

The weather, rivers and waves all break up rocks. As the pieces of rock get smaller, they become a mix of rocks and sand.

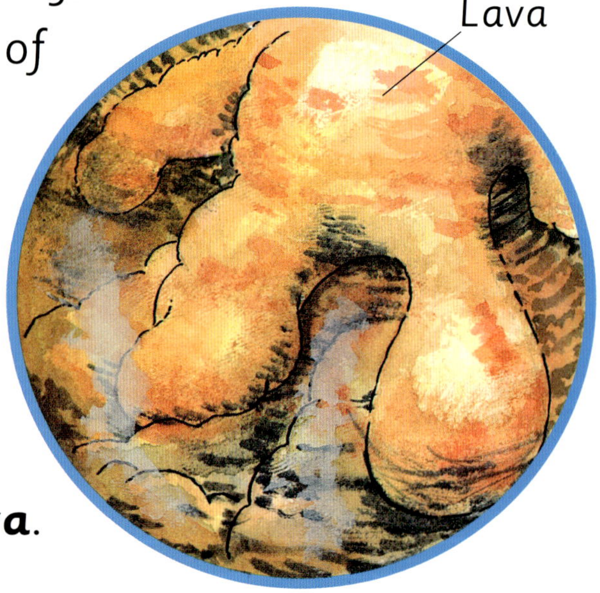

Volcano

Red hot liquid rock, called magma, lies deep under the Earth's crust. A volcano is formed when magma explodes through the crust and pours over the ground as **lava**.

WHAT'S IN THE SOIL?

Dig up some soil and put it in a sieve. Shake the sieve over a bucket. Tip the soil left in the sieve onto white paper and spread it out. It is made up of stones, bits of plants, shells and even small animals.

MAKE A RIVER

Do this activity outside.

Place a pile of earth on a large tray to make a mountain. Bury some big and small stones in the pile. Slowly pour water on top of the mountain. Watch the water turn into a river, running between the stones. It carries soil downhill and makes a lake at the bottom. What happens to the buried stones?

DISCOVER HOW MOUNTAINS ARE FORMED

Huge plates in the Earth's crust crash together. They push up the rock in between them and form mountains.

Spread a tablecloth over the whole of a table. Push the material together with your hands to make mountains and **valleys**.

Weather

Sunshine and showers, snow, wind and storms are all different kinds of weather. Sometimes the weather makes us feel hot, sometimes it makes us feel very cold.

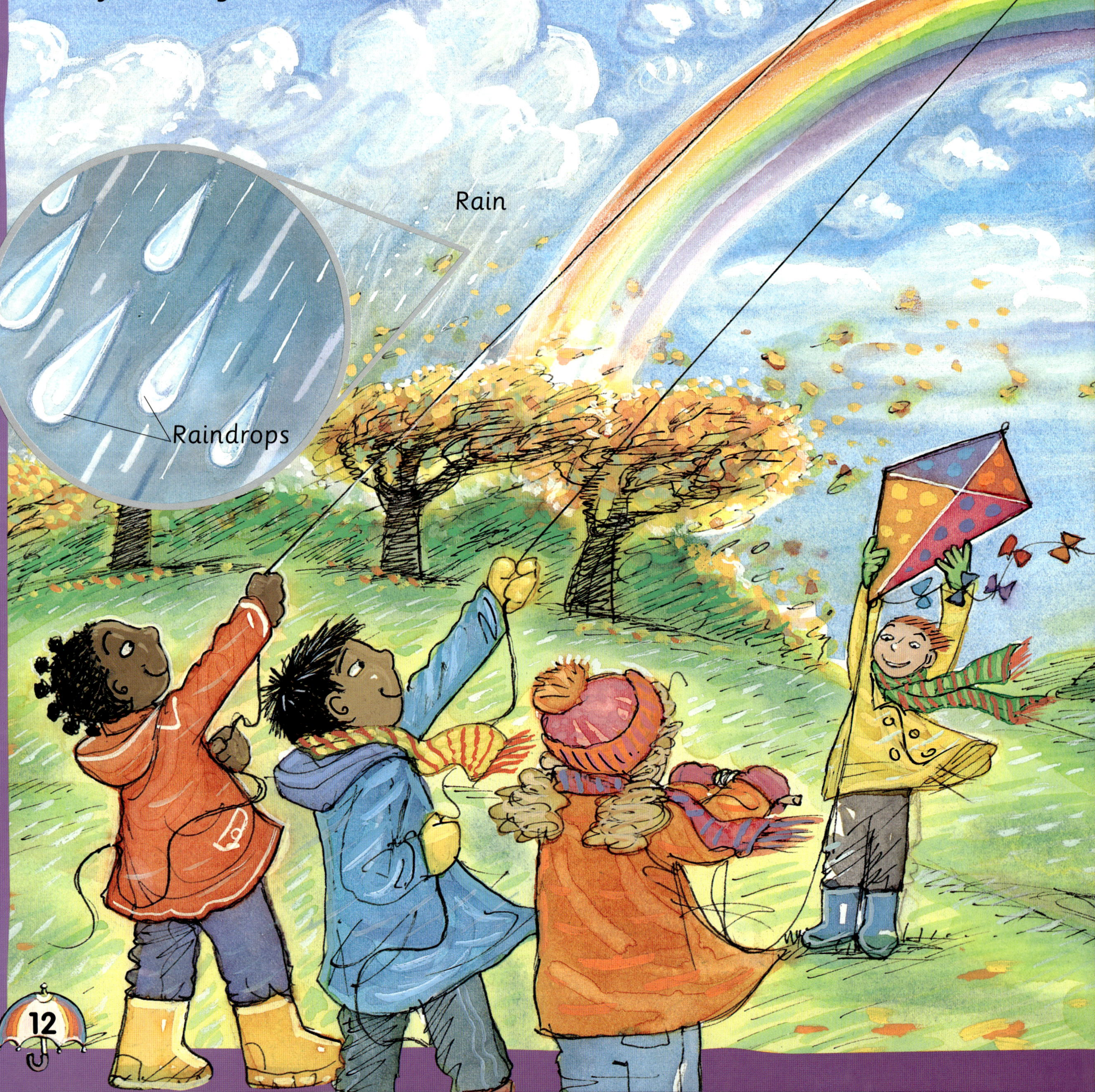

Sun
Lightning
Rain clouds
Rainbow
PICTURE SEARCH
★ search for clues that the wind is blowing
★ search for different shaped clouds

Sunshine and showers

When sunlight shines through raindrops, it is split into seven colours and you see a **rainbow**.

The water cycle

Water is never lost because it goes around between land, sea and air. We call the way water goes around, the water cycle.

1 Condensation

Water vapour turns into tiny water droplets in the cold air.

2 Clouds

Water droplets collect and form clouds.

3 Rain

Water droplets join together and fall to the ground as rain.

4 Evaporation

Water turns into a gas called water vapour and rises into the air.

MAKE A PINWHEEL

Draw a dot in the middle of a square of card. Draw 2 lines diagonally across the card to the corners. Colour in each piece in rainbow colours. Cut along the lines. Bend the right side of each corner into the middle of the card. Push a pin through all the corners and into a stick.

Run with your pinwheel and watch it spin. What happens to the colours?

WHAT IS EVAPORATION?

Make a mixture of salt and water and pour it into a saucer. Put the saucer on a window ledge in hot sunlight. The water will **evaporate** – turn into water vapour – and leave the salt behind.

MAKE RAINBOWS

Blow *bubbles* outside on a sunny day. Sunlight splits as it shines through the *bubbles'* soapy skins and makes tiny rainbows.

Moon

The moon is a ball of rock in space. It **orbits** the Earth. At night, the moon seems to shine with a pale, silvery light.

Earth
Lunar module
PICTURE SEARCH
★ look for craters and different shaped rocks
★ look for things that have arrived from Earth
Moon crater
Moon rocks

Visiting the moon

There is no air on the moon. **Astronauts** who visit the moon carry tanks of air to breathe.

Gravity

Gravity is the force that pulls you down towards the ground. Gravity is so weak on the moon that astronauts float off the ground when they walk. They have heavy weights in their boots to pull them down to the surface.

Phases of the moon

As the moon orbits the Earth it looks as though it changes shape. In fact, some parts are in sunlight and other parts are in shadow.

New moon

Crescent moon

Full moon

Half moon

DAY AND NIGHT

Draw a picture of yourself on a piece of cardboard. Stick the figure onto your model of Earth (see page 7). You will need a friend to help you. In a dark room, shine a torch onto the ball. Spin the ball around. See how you move from light – day time – into shadow – night time.

REFLECTED LIGHT

Moonlight is pale because it is **reflected light** from the sun. Use a crumpled ball of white paper for the moon and a torch for the sun.

Draw a picture and stick it inside a shoe box. Then in a dark room, shine a torch into the box. How well can you see the picture?

Dangle your moon in front of the box and shine a torch on it. It casts a pale light on the picture. Keep the torch on and take the moon away. The picture will be in the dark because there is no moon to reflect light onto it.

Planets

Our Earth is one of nine planets that orbit the sun. Planets are balls of rock. We see them shining at night because, like the moon, they reflect sunlight.

Sun
Mercury
Venus
Earth
Mars
Asteroid belt
Jupiter
Jupiter's red spot
Asteroids
PICTURE SEARCH
★ look for the nine planets
★ look for planets with rings

Exploring the planets

We know what the planets look like because of **space probes** such as Voyager 2. They send information about the planets back to Earth.

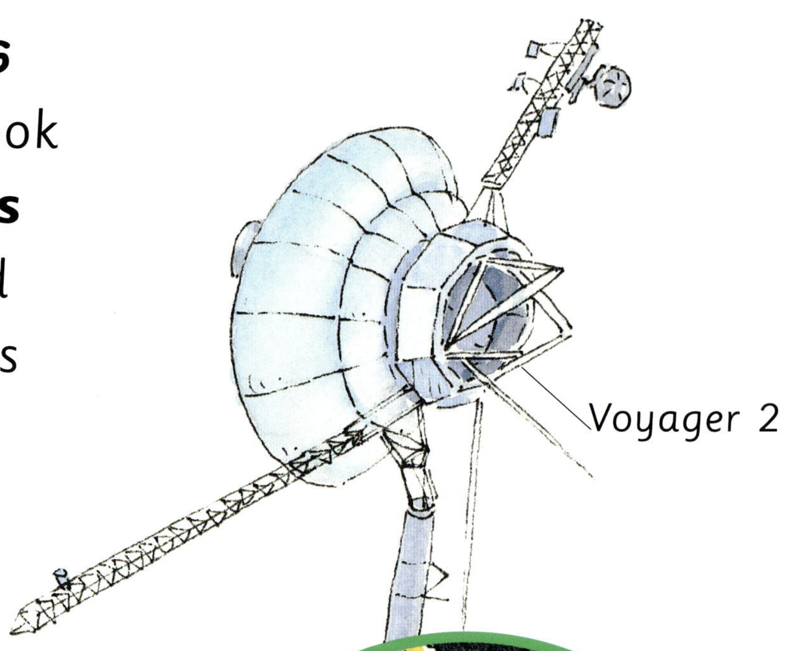

Asteroid belt

A band of space rocks called the **asteroid belt** orbits the sun between Mars and Jupiter.

Saturn's rings

Saturn's colourful rings are made up of millions of pieces of frozen rock.

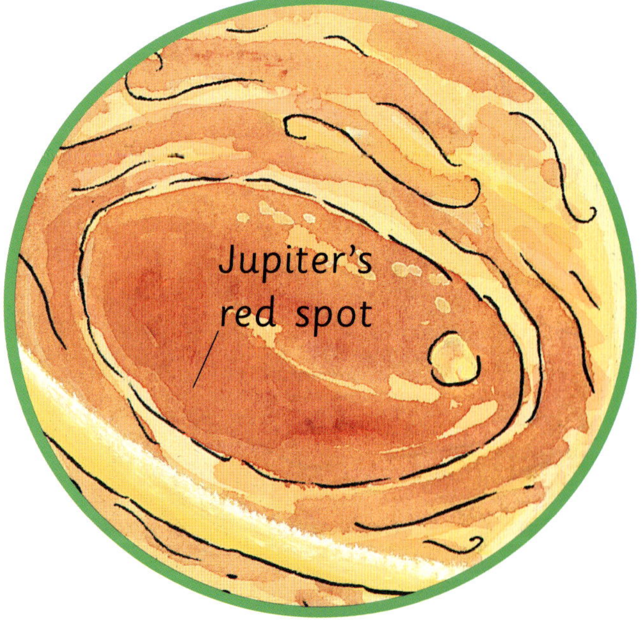

Great red spot

The great red spot on Jupiter is probably a gigantic storm. The red spot is twice as wide as the Earth.

GO INTO ORBIT

Push a tennis ball into the toe of an old pop sock. In an open space, hold the end of the sock and swing the ball around.

WARNING: Make sure there's no one close to you when you swing your sock.

Imagine you are the sun. The ball is like a planet orbiting the sun. The pop sock holds the ball in place as you swing it around.

MAKE A BALLOON SPACE ROCKET

Burning gases from the rocket engine thrust the rocket away from Earth and into space.

Turn a balloon into a space rocket. With a friend, blow up a balloon each and let them go. Air inside the balloons escapes very fast and pushes them along.

Whose balloon whizzes through the air the longest?

Stars

On a clear night you can see lots of stars twinkling in the sky. Like the sun, stars are enormous balls of burning gas.

Milky way
Galaxy
PICTURE SEARCH
★ look for the Milky Way stretching across the sky
★ look for patterns made by the stars
Shooting star

The night sky

Stars twinkle because their light has to travel to Earth through specks of dirt and droplets of water in the **atmosphere**.

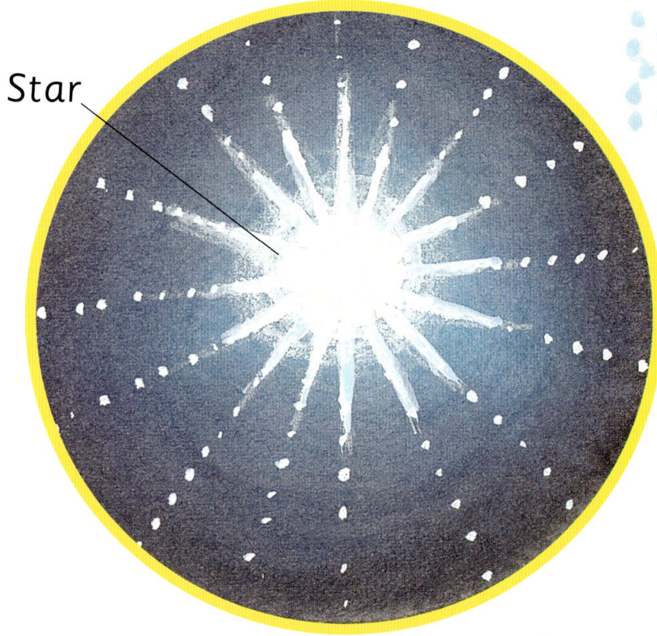

Stars

Stars are so far away, their light can take millions of years to travel through space to reach Earth.

Galaxy

A **galaxy** is a group of billions of stars. The stars in some galaxies are grouped together in the shape of a spiral.

Milky Way

On a clear night, you can see some of the billions of stars that are in our galaxy which is called the **Milky Way**.

TRACKING STARS

As the Earth spins around, the stars seem to move across the sky.

At night, stick some tracing paper on a window from which you can see stars. Draw an outline of the horizon. Mark the brightest star. Then mark it again an hour later – it will have changed position.

MAKE A TELESCOPE

Stand a magnifying make-up mirror so it reflects the stars. Hold a small mirror so it reflects the stars from the magnifying mirror. Now look at the stars in the small mirror through a magnifying glass – they will look much bigger.

Hubble telescope

The Hubble telescope orbits Earth. Earth's atmosphere **blurs** our view of the stars. Hubble takes clear pictures of the stars because it moves above the atmosphere.

More to learn about the stars

Constellations

When we look up at the stars, we can see them in patterns called **constellations**. Long ago the Greeks named constellations after characters from their stories.

The Great Bear (Ursa Major) and the Little Bear (Ursa Minor) were a mother and son. They were turned into bears by the god Zeus.

Northern stars

The Great Dog (Canis Major) was named after a dog said to be the fastest creature on Earth.

The Pole Star or Polaris, sits above the North Pole. Travellers use Polaris to help them find their way.

Sirius, or the Dog Star, is the brightest star in the night sky (Sirius is part of Canis Major).

Southern stars

Centaurus is a centaur – a creature that is half man and half horse.

The Southern Cross points to the South Pole. It guides sailors across the ocean.

BE A STAR GAZER

- Choose a clear night with no clouds. Avoid bright lights.
- Look carefully. You will see more stars as your eyes get used to the dark..
- Watch out for things that are moving. They might be an aeroplane or even a **satellite**.

You need:

- Binoculars are better than a telescope because you use both eyes.
- Something to lean the binoculars on – the back of a garden chair or a wall – to hold them steady.
- A pocket guide and a torch for checking what you see.

Be careful

- Dress warmly – it gets cold at night.
- Don't walk around looking through binoculars or just looking up – you can easily bump into things.

Glossary

Air
Air is all around us but we can't see it. It is made up of gases including oxygen and water vapour. Living things need air to breathe.

Asteroid belt
Asteroids are pieces of rock in space. Thousands of asteroids are moving around the sun between the planets Mars and Jupiter make up the asteroid belt.

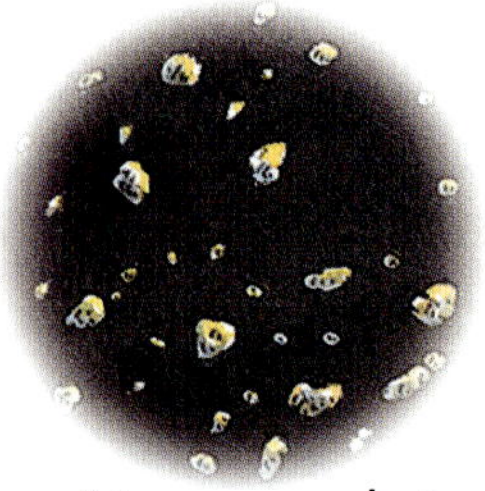

Astronaut
An astronaut is a person who travels into space to explore it.

Atmosphere
The atmosphere is a layer of air and dust. It surrounds planet Earth helping to keep it warm and protecting it from the harmful rays of the sun.

Condensation
Water vapour is a gas in the air. Condensation takes place when air cools and water vapour changes into droplets of water.

Constellations
When you look up at the stars, some seem to be grouped together in patterns. We call these patterns constellations.

Crust
A crust is the outside coating of something, such as the crust of a loaf of bread. The Earth's crust is a layer of rock.

Evaporation
When water is heated it evaporates. This means it changes into an invisible gas called water vapour in the air.

Fossil
Fossils form when a plant or animal dies and is covered by layers of sand or soil that harden into rock. After millions of years, we can see the shape of the plant or animal in the rock.

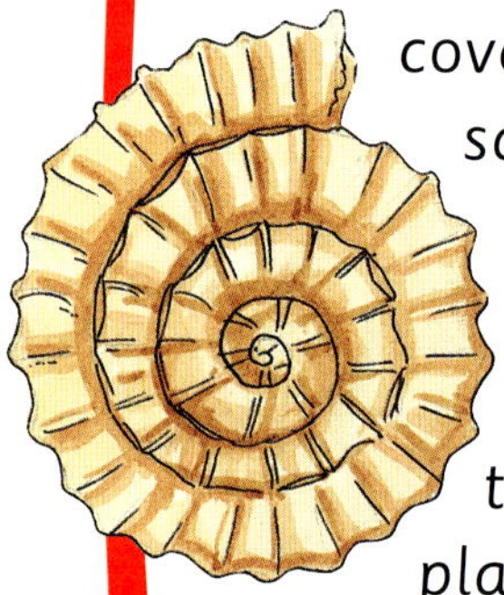

Galaxy
A galaxy is a group of billions of stars. There are billions of galaxies in space.

Gravity
Gravity is the force that pulls objects towards each other. Earth's gravity pulls everything towards its centre. The Sun's gravity pulls the planets towards it.

Lava

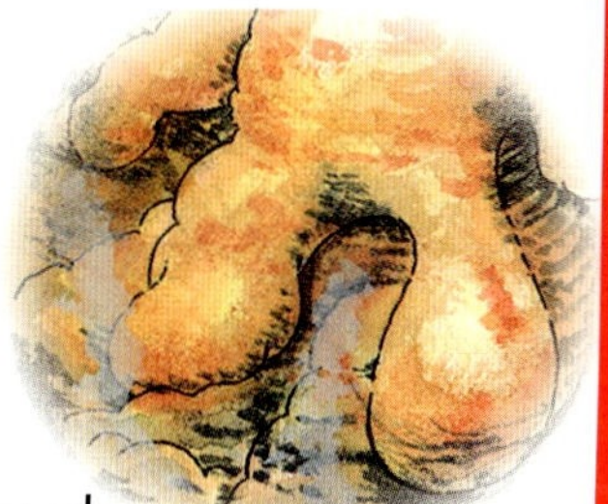

Lava is a red hot flowing liquid that bursts through the Earth's crust to form a volcano. When lava cools, it becomes solid rock.

Milky Way

The Milky Way is the name of the group of stars that make up the galaxy that our nearest star, the sun, belongs to.

Orbit

An orbit is the path an object takes as it moves around another object. For example, the moon orbits Earth and Earth orbits the sun.

Plains

Plains are huge areas of flat land with no hills or valleys.

Phases of the moon

As the moon moves around Earth it seems to change shape. We call these changes the phases of the moon.

Rainbow

A rainbow is the colourful bow we see in the sky when sunlight shines through raindrops and splits into the seven colours of the spectrum – red, orange, yellow, green, light blue, dark blue, purple.

Reflected light

The moon does not give out light of its own. When sunlight shines on the moon, it reflects the light as if it were a mirror. Moonlight is reflected light from the sun.

Satellite

A satellite is a man-made object sent from Earth into space where it orbits the Earth. Satellites are used to send signals from one part of Earth to another.

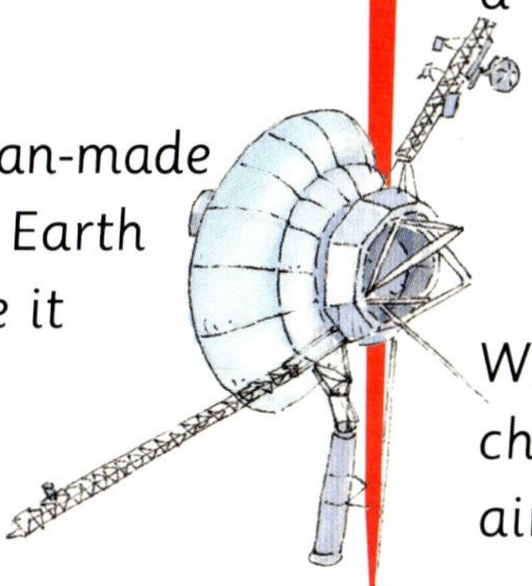

Space probes

Space probes are satellites, telescopes and any spacecraft sent from Earth to explore space, that send back information.

Tilted

When something is tilted it leans to one side. Earth is tilted in space. This means that one of the Earth's poles is always leaning towards the sun.

Valley

Valleys are the dips between mountains and hills. Rivers can carve out valleys in the rock as they flow down towards the sea.

Volcano

A volcano is a crack or hole in the Earth's crust. Hot liquid rock called lava flows out and forms a hill or a mountain.

Water vapour

When water is heated, it changes into a gas in the air called water vapour.

Index